Chris Buckton
Anne Sanderson

Series editor: Leonie Bennett

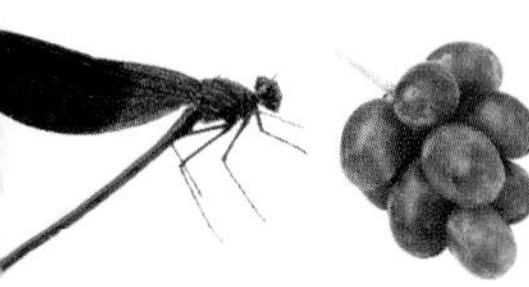   

Symbols

PCM A photocopy master is available to support differentiation.

Differentiation symbols.

1 Easy to complete.

2 All pupils complete activity. Activities are supported by a PCM for extra help.

3 More difficult activites.

Author Team: Chris Buckton
Anne Sanderson
Series Editor: Leonie Bennett

Ginn
Linacre House, Jordan Hill, Oxford, OX2 8DP
a division of Reed Educational and Professional Publishing Ltd
www.ginn.co.uk

ISBN 0602 296846

04 03 02 01
10 9 8 7 6 5 4 3 2

Designed and produced by Gecko Ltd, Bicester, Oxon
Cover design by Gecko Ltd, Bicester, Oxon
Printed in Spain by Edelvives

Contents

1

CHARACTER SKETCHES

A Giant of a Man

1 A giant of a man with a face like a ham and a mass of rust-coloured hair that sprouted in a tangle all over the top of his head. In his hand he held a long yellow cane which curved round like the top of a walking stick.

From *Boy* by Roald Dahl

2 She was a small skinny old hag with a moustache on her upper lip and a mouth as sour as a green gooseberry. She never smiled. Her apron was grey and greasy. Her blouse had bits of breakfast all over it, toast-crumbs and tea stains and splotches of dried egg-yolk.

From *Keeping Henry* by Nina Bawden

small details

adjectives

3 She was a tiny, quick, delicate person who hardly ever stopped working and never stopped talking, hopping from one thing to another so fast it was sometimes hard to keep up with her. Her bright blue eyes snapped with laughter.

From *Boy* by Roald Dahl

powerful verbs

4 Mr Jones was a quiet man, a bit stooped over and tired looking. Sometimes he would suck the ends of his long, drooping moustache and sigh, but mostly he just sat, very still, very silent.

From *Keeping Henry* by Nina Bawden

Reading

Work with a partner.

1. Read the character sketch on **sheet 1**. Complete the sentences.

2. Read the character sketch on **sheet 2**. Complete the sentences.

Writing

PCM 4

Work with a partner.

1. Plan your characters together. Brainstorm one sympathetic and one unsympathetic character.
2. Begin to write a description of each one.

Don't forget!
Make sure the small details make your characters seem real.

Extended Writing

1. Revise your work. Make a best copy – add a drawing. Give your characters names.
2. Write a short story with your characters in.

Helping Each Other

How helpful is my partner?

If I work with a friend I get more ideas for my writing. I like to get help from someone my own age.

My response partner hurts my feelings by saying my stories are rubbish. But he doesn't say which bits or how to get it better.

My partner is good at saying what he doesn't understand, so I know the bits I need to add.

I don't like it when all the comments are about things that are wrong.

What is my writing for?

I like my writing going up on the wall.

It's good if you can get to take your work home.

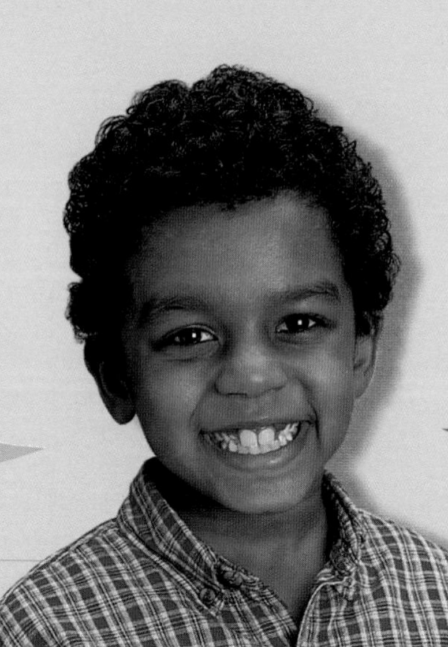

I really like it when we write to a real person.

I like making books for the little ones.

If I read my story to someone else it helps me see my faults.

I find it useful to use a chart like this.

I like ______________________

____

____

I like ______________________

____

____

I suggest ______________________

____

Reading

How can you help each other before, during and after you write?

Talk through the questionnaire on **sheet 5**.

Fill in the questionnaire.

Writing

Work with a partner.

1. What tips would you give your response partner? Brainstorm some ideas. Make notes on **sheet 6**.
2. Write out each tip as a sentence.
3. Talk about how you will present your work. It could be a poster or booklet.

Extended Writing

Carry on writing and revising your tips. Make a final book or poster.

Don't forget!
INSTRUCTIONS:
use the present tense
put the verb first

3

STORY PLANNING

The Magic Shoes

One day, one normal day, Paul was taking a stroll on the beach. As he scanned the horizon he became aware of something glittering in the sand. It was a pair of old shoes. They looked just his size so he decided to put them on. Just as he inserted his foot into the left shoe he heard a muffled, squeaky voice. 'Hey, you're squashing me,' it said.

Hurridly he took them off. A thin purple line shot into the sky and back down came a small genie. 'Who are you?' exclaimed Paul.

'I am the Genie of the Shoes,' it boomed.

It seemed to grow very tall and let out a huge peal of laughter and promptly shrunk to its original size.

'Can't never get un roight,' it said in a slightly Birmingham accent.

'Are you the type of Genie that grants you three wishes?' Paul asked.

'Yep,' it answered.

'Great! Now, I'd like to . . .'

'Hang on, you gotta address me proper.'

'Right, Genie of the Shoes, grant me these three wishes. Number 1, make me fly.'

As his feet lifted off the ground he began to shout. 'Help, I wish I was on the ground again.'

He hit the ground with a thump.

'Huh, fat use this is,' Paul said.

'Go and bother someone else. I wish you were back in your shoes and somewhere you can't bother me.'

The genie was sucked into the shoes and they began to take off and fly over the sea until they were a dot in the distance and vanished.

'Oh well, now I can get on with a normal life,' said Paul.

John, age 9

Reading

Work as a group.

1. Look at the object on your table. Brainstorm ideas for a story about it.
2. Make a spider diagram of all your ideas.

Writing

Use your spider diagram to plan a story. Use **sheet 7** to help you.

Extended Writing

Use your plan to write the first draft of your story.
Discuss your story with your partner as you write. Ask your partner to comment on your draft as you revise it.

- Introduction
- Build-up
- Climax
- Resolution

4

PLAYSCRIPT

Fantastic Mr Fox

Scene 1

BOGGIS, BUNCE and BEAN are seated at three tables laden with food and placed in a line on stage in front of the drawn curtains. They are 'frozen'. Lights are off at this point. Children enter from the back of the hall [spotlight]. They skip, run and laugh up the centre aisle, chanting:

set the scene

Children: Boggis and Bunce and Bean,
One fat, one short, one lean,
These horrible crooks,
So different in looks,
Were none the less equally mean.

stage directions

[Children sit on steps at front of stage. As each farmer is mentioned, a spotlight pans on to him and he becomes alive, eating or drinking revoltingly.]

First child: Let's sit down a minute.

Second child: What shall we do? We could go up to the woods and play.

no speech marks

Third child: Or we could go down to the river.

First child: Better not. My mum says I'm not to go anywhere near the valley 'cos of those three nasty men. You know the ones – they're always talking together in low whispers and looking over their shoulders to see if anyone's listening. The dreaded Boggis, Bunce and Bean, no less.

character's name

Second child: My mum says the same. She says not only are they the nastiest farmers in the whole county, they're also the richest. They never spend any money and they pay miserable wages to everyone who works for them. They store all the money they get from selling their chickens and ducks and geese in great padlocked chests.

Third child: Which do you think is the worst?

Second child: Don't know. They've all got such horrible habits. [*Laughter*]

Extract from *Fantastic Mr Fox: A Play* by Roald Dahl and Sally Reid

Reading

Work in groups. Prepare a performance of the play. Use **sheet 8**.

1. Who will read the parts of the first, second and third child?
2. Talk about *how* you will read each part. Make notes on the playscript to remind you.
3. Practise reading your playscript aloud together.

Writing

Write Scene 2 of **Fantastic Mr Fox**.
Mark the story on **sheet 10** to help you.

Extended Writing

Finish writing your playscript. Read it through as a group. You can add some stage directions.

NEWSPAPER REPORT

Feathers Fly!

catchy headline

FEATHERS FLY ON LOCAL FARMS

By Rashid Patel

sum up the events

Police are investigating a series of attacks on three poultry farms in the area.

According to local farmers, Boggis, Bunce and Bean, the thief is almost certainly a cunning fox that lives above the valley in a wood. So far attempts to catch the thief have failed, in spite of the farmers setting traps to catch him.

Farmer Bunce today told our reporter, "If I catch that fox, I'll put a bullet through his head." This seems to be the feeling of the other two farmers in the area.

quotes

Farmer Bean is setting up a Fox Watch, and is appealing to local residents to come and help. Anybody wishing to join should call 324447 as soon as possible.

Reading

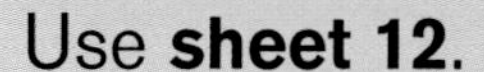

Use **sheet 12**.

1. Tick the items you might find in a newspaper report.
2. What questions would you ask Farmer Bean?
3. Write the headline as a longer sentence.

Writing

1. Plan your own newspaper report. It could be about a real event, or an event from a story. Brainstorm ideas and make notes on **sheet 14**.
2. Write a punchy headline.
3. Begin to write your first draft.

Don't forget!

- sum up the events
- use quotes
- include facts
- make people want to read on

Extended Writing

1. Finish drafting your report. Edit and revise your work with a partner.
2. Write out the final version. Include a big, bold heading and a picture. Lay it out in columns.

6

HISTORICAL NOVEL

The Evacuee

That weekend the 'vaccies' arrived from Liverpool. A coachload of them, pale and miserable, clutching cardboard suitcases, name labels tied to their coats.

Tom's mum was sorry for them. She wanted to take in a boy or girl, but the house was too crowded. Widow Robertson, though, was on her own. She took an evacuee and the whole street knew about it.

'It's a crying shame. Those snobs up Birch Lane looked the poor jiggers up and down and picked out the cleanest ones. When it was all done, this poor little chap was left.'

Poor little chap? He was the same age as Tom, but hard as nails, Tom could see that, with a face like a ferret, a sharp nose and red eyes. He came out into the street just as the gang met up. William, who seemed to be in a good mood again, winked and raised his voice.

'Yeah, you know where Liverpool is – that little place across the Mersey from New Brighton.'

The evacuee rose to the bait.

'It's on the map, any road, not like this dump. There's nothing here, no flicks, two shops, a load of fields and a bunch of useless cows.'

'Our cows aren't useless,' said William loftily.

'What use are they?'

'They give good milk, that's what.'

The Liverpool lad stared in disbelief.

'Don't be gormless. You don't get milk from those mucky things. It comes clean in bottles, round our way.'

The gang burst into laughter, punching each other. Even Molly, who felt sorry for him, had to grin.

The pale face reddened. He picked on Tom, who was his own size.

'What are you laughing at?'

Tom choked, and said hastily, 'Nowt, mate.'

'It had better be nowt, kidder.' The evacuee's tone was menacing. He turned on his heels and went into Widow Robertson's entry.

William looked scornfully at Tom. 'Fancy letting a Scouser talk to you like that. You should've poked him one.'

'Oh, forget it,' said Molly hastily. But William was not going to forget.

An extract from *Tom's Private War* by Robert Leeson

Reading

1 Fill in the gaps in these sentences:

> The evacuees travelled by .... from Liverpool.
> (car, coach, train, aeroplane)
> The people in Birch Lane picked the .... children.
> (first, happiest, cleanest)

2 How did William annoy the evacuee?

3 Why did the evacuee pick on Tom?

4 Think of some adjectives to describe William, Molly and the evacuee. Use **sheet 16** to help you.

Writing

Imagine you are an evacuee during World War 2. You can use the events from the story or make something up.

Write two paragraphs about your experience.

PCM 18

Extended Writing

1. Plan a short story in which you are an evacuee. Include your description of how you felt.
2. Write a first draft. Try to include some dialogue.

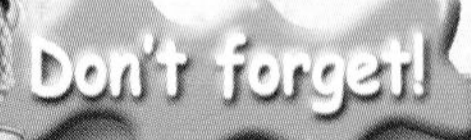

- **Write in the first person.**
- **How would you feel?**
- **What would you do?**
- **What would you say?**

7

PARAGRAPHS

Up and Away!

Maybe none of it would have happened if Philip had listened to his father's warning not to play with the kite on his own. Maybe. But who can tell with magic?

5 "It's big enough to blow you away," his mother said when she saw the kite.

Philip laughed. Nobody had ever been blown away on a kite – not even one as huge as this. His uncle had brought it back as a present from China 10 and it really was the biggest and best you've ever seen. It was shaped like a dragon and was coloured red, yellow and green.

Philip wanted to go out and fly it at once but his father said he had to wait until the weekend. The 15 weekend! That was four whole days away.

Philip put the kite in the corner of his bedroom. Every time he looked at it, he heard a voice whispering in his head.

"Go on," the voice said, "it's your kite. Dad's just a 20 spoil-sport. Go on – it'll be good fun. No one will know if you just sneak out for half an hour."

For two days, Philip managed to say 'no' to the voice, but on the third day he gave in.

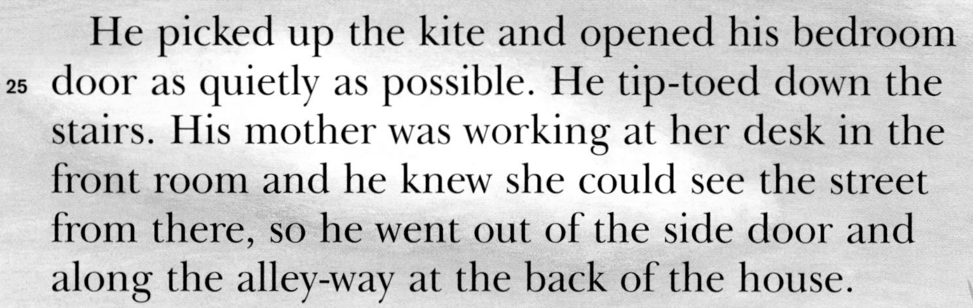

He picked up the kite and opened his bedroom door as quietly as possible. He tip-toed down the stairs. His mother was working at her desk in the front room and he knew she could see the street from there, so he went out of the side door and along the alley-way at the back of the house.

The kite was so big that his arms ached from holding it up so that it didn't touch the ground. It was so big that by the time he reached the top of the hill in the park he was out of breath.

Then, after all that, there wasn't even the slightest breeze. For a quarter of an hour, he ran up and down trying to make the kite fly, but each time it just flapped back to the ground. After one final go, he gave up. He wrapped the string into a ball and bent down to pick up the kite.

A little puff of wind blew his hair. He looked up. A small, round, black cloud was racing across the blue sky. It was moving faster than any cloud Philip had ever seen. He felt the kite move in his hand. The long dragon's tail wagged from side to side like a dog's when it sees a friend.

Then, out of nowhere came the wind. Whistling and spinning and howling. Philip closed his eyes. He felt his arms rise above him as the wind caught the kite and lifted it up. When he opened his eyes, he was already twenty feet above the ground and rising fast. Straight up. He watched the top of the hill grow smaller and smaller until it was just a green dot below.

An extract from *Beaver Towers* by Nigel Hinton

Reading

Write a short caption to say what each paragraph is about. Use **sheet 19**.

Writing

1. Plan your own story about Philip's adventure with the kite. Organise the events into paragraphs. Use **sheet 21** to help you.
2. Begin to write the first draft of your story. Keep to your plan!

Extended Writing

1. Finish drafting your story. Keep the ending in mind so that you can lead up to it.
2. Swap your first draft with a partner. Suggest how each others' work can be improved.

Don't forget!

PARAGRAPHS:

- organise events
- give chunks of information
- keep the story moving

Cats sleep fat

Catalog

Cats sleep fat and walk thin.
Cats, when they sleep, slump;
When they wake, pull in –
And where the plump's been
There's skin.
Cats walk thin.

Cats wait in a lump,
Jump in a streak.
Cats, when they jump, are sleek
As a grape slipping its skin –
They have technique.
Oh, cats don't creak.
They sneak.

From 'Catalog' by Rosalie Moore

Cat Kenning

Eye-shiner
Fur-smoother
Mouse-catcher
Bird-hunter
Bed-nicker
Fish-taker
Whisker-bristler
Tail-twitcher
Lap-leaper

Gemma, age 8

I see a cat

I see a cat
Poised to pounce
Eyes stare still and hard as jewels
Crouched like a coiled spring
Frozen concentration
Only a flicker
A tail like a finger beckoning
At an ignorant mouse
Suddenly it strikes.

Akbar, age 9

Reading

1. Read each poem aloud with your partner. Which is your favourite? Complete the following sentences:

   The poem I like best is .... because ....

   The line in this poem I like best is .... because ....

2. Compare your answers with your partner. Do you agree?

Writing

Write your own animal poem.

1. Try to picture the animal clearly. What does it look like? What does it do? How does it move?
2. Write your first draft.
3. Swap your draft with a partner. Talk about how you could improve it. Help each other to revise your drafts.

PCM 23

Extended Writing

Finish revising your poem and write out the final version neatly. Illustrate it with pictures or photographs.

Don't forget!

- make your animal seem real
- powerful verbs
- good ending

MAGAZINE REPORT

Young Archaeologist

JUNIOR REPORTER

This summer, Claire went on holiday to the island of Cyprus. There she found a wealth of ancient treasures. Here is her report.

Cyprus – The Island of Aphrodite

Cyprus is known as the island of Aphrodite. Aphrodite is the Greek goddess of love.

There is a rock on the island where she is supposed to have been born. It is said that if you swim around this rock three times at midnight – with no clothes on – you will be granted eternal youth.

facts

I stayed in the town of Paphos, which used to be a mini kingdom and is rich in history. There are beautiful mosaics in some of the houses. The colours are still very vivid even though most of the mosaics were made in the Roman period. In the town there is also a 2nd century Odeon – which is a Greek theatre.

present tense

Paphos is an amazing place and I recommend it to all archaeology fans.

Competition

We have 10 copies of the new edition of *1066 and All That*, to give away to the first lucky readers who match these events to the correct dates.

1. Claudius invades Britain
2. Hitler comes to power in Germany
3. The Battle of Hastings
4. Charles I executed

1933 1649 1066 43

Send your answers on a postcard to:

YAC Competition, Bowes Morrell House, 111 Walmgate, York YO1 9WA

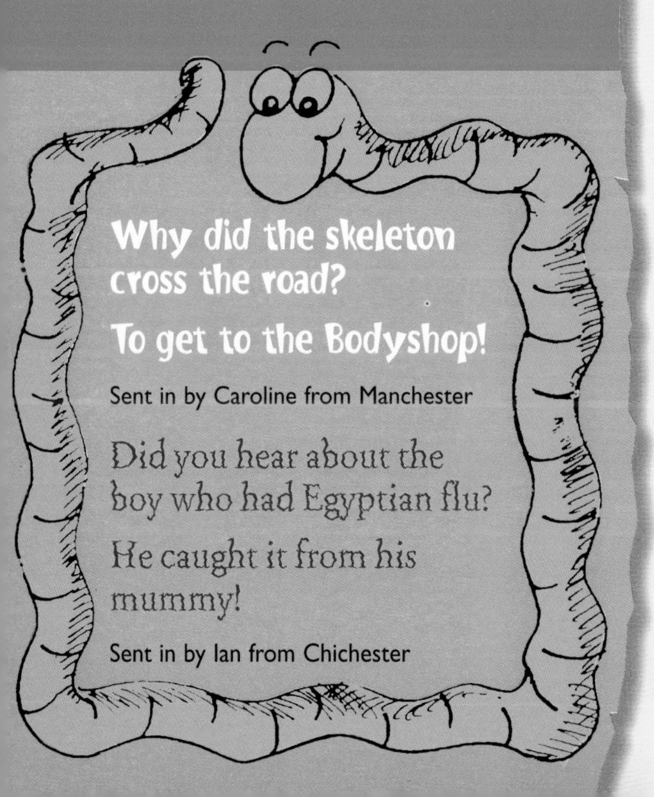

Why did the skeleton cross the road?
To get to the Bodyshop!
Sent in by Caroline from Manchester
Did you hear about the boy who had Egyptian flu?
He caught it from his mummy!
Sent in by Ian from Chichester

Reading

1. Who do you thing think reads the *Young Archaeologist*?
   - **a** adults **b** children ages 5–8
   - **c** children aged 9–16

   People who are interested in:
   - **a** travel
   - **b** finding out about the past
   - **c** mosaics **d** competitions
2. Which are the three main headings.
3. Why does Claire recommend Paphos to archaeology fans?

Writing

Work in pairs.

Draft a report for the class magazine. Use books and other sources to find more information if you need to.

Extended Writing

1. Finish your draft report. Read it through with a partner and make any changes.
2. Produce the final version as a magazine article. Give it a catchy heading. Add some jokes or a competition.

10

MOOD AND FEELING

A Wolf in Me

adverbs

I have a deer in me
Lying down shyly
Peacefully waiting
Quietly watching
Walking past invisibly
Nobody looking at her
Nobody knows her
But she doesn't care

by Yolande

verbs

I have a beetle in me
It scurries and scrabbles
It tickles and shrills
It pokes and prods
It mummers and whispers
It itches and aggravates
People want to stamp on it

by Jeffrey

Reading

Work with a partner.

1. Talk about the poems together. Which one do you like best? Why? Do you both agree?
2. Fill in the comments on **sheet 25**.

Writing

Write your own 'mood' poem.

1. Talk with a partner about your poem. What mood are you going to write about? What animal fits the mood? What could it be doing?
2. Talk about how you might end your poem.
3. Use the ideas you have talked about to draft your own 'mood' poem.

Don't forget!

ADVERBS:

- add to the meaning of the verb
- affect the mood
- usually end in -ly

Extended Writing

1. Finish your first draft. Read it to your partner.
2. Revise the poem and write a final version.

DIRECTIONS

Weekend Bike Ride

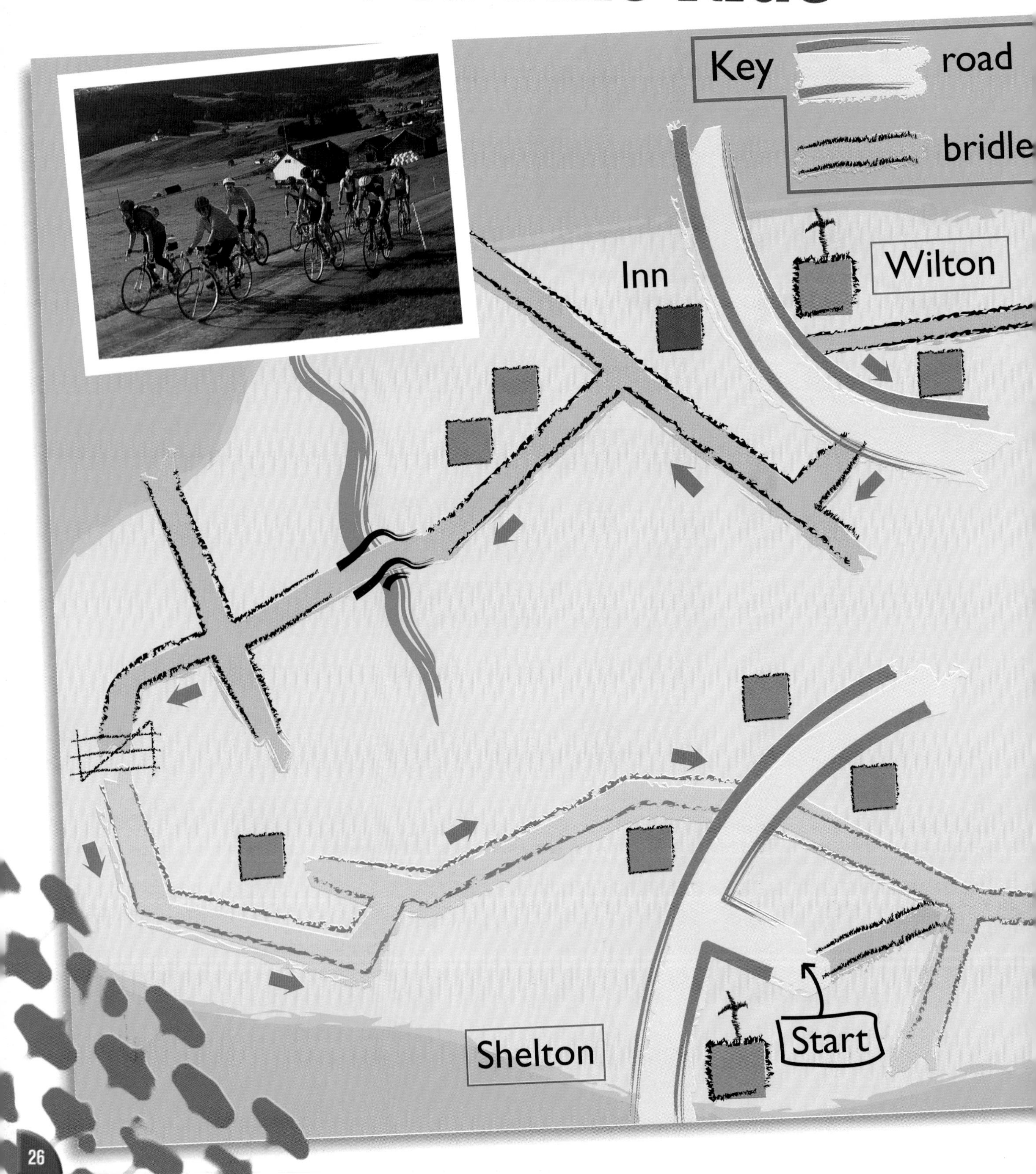

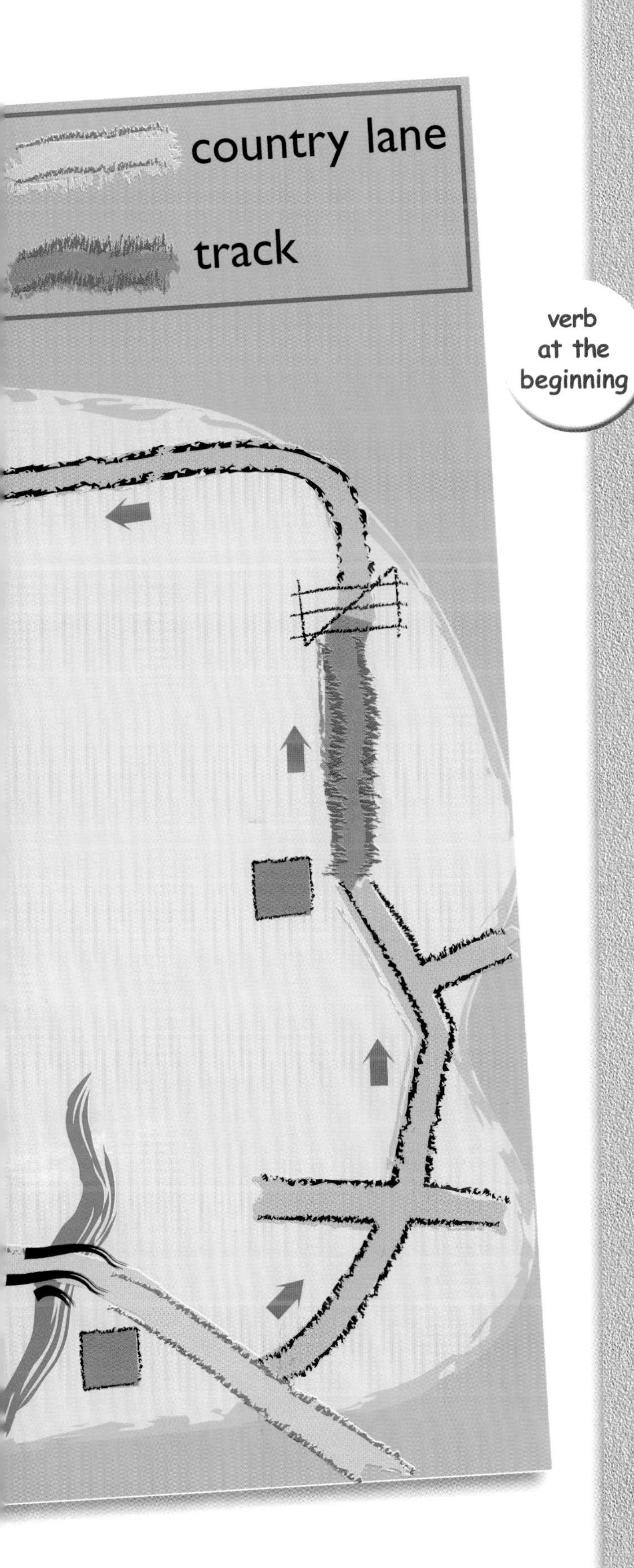

This bike ride is about 9 km long.

You will need an all-terrain bike because some of the paths are muddy. Don't take a dog with you because you will go near a field with sheep in it.

verb at the beginning

Start by the church in Shelton. Go along the road for about 100 m. Then turn right down Church Walk. When you get to the lane, turn right. Go over a bridge.

gives an idea of distance

After about ½ km you'll see a house on your right and a bridlepath sign on your left. Follow the bridlepath along the edge of the field. Ride slowly, as the track is quite bumpy here.

Go past the cottage on your left. When you get to the gate remember to shut it behind you. Ride carefully along the next field watching out for potholes.

At the church in Wilton, turn left along the main road. Or you could stop for a rest and have a sandwich at the inn along the main road to your right.

Reading

Work with a partner.

1. Write directions for the rest of the bike ride. Number your instructions 1 to 5.

2. One of you read out the directions while the other follows them on the map. Are they clear and easy to follow? Make any changes.

Writing

Work with a partner.

1. Write a first draft of some directions for a local walk.
2. Test your directions as you work. Read them through with your partner. How easy are they to follow?

Extended Writing

1. Finish drafting and revising your directions.
2. Draw your own map to go with them. Include arrows and a key.

DIRECTIONS:

- use short clear sentences beginning with a verb
- number the stages
- things to look out for along the way
- give an idea of how far it is

12

DESCRIPTION

The Iron Woman

Ted Hughes

In this story an Iron Woman comes to take revenge on humans for polluting the seas, lakes and rivers.

One perfectly ordinary day, Lucy is walking home across the marshes on her way back from school, when she feels the earth begin to shake…

The marsh was always a lonely place. Now she felt the loneliness. As she stood there, looking up, the whole bluish and pinky sky of soft cloud moved slowly. She looked again at the long
5 drain, where the reeds leaned all one way, bowing gently in the light wind. The eel was no longer to be seen. Was it still writhing and bobbing its head up, as the slow flow carried it away through the marsh? She looked down into the drain, under
10 the bridge. The black water moved silently, crumpling and twirling little whorls of light.

Then it came again. Beneath her feet the bridge road jumped and the rail jarred her hand. At the same moment, the water
15 surface of the drain was blurred by a sudden mesh of tiny ripples all over it.

short sentences

An earthquake! It must be an earthquake.

A completely new kind of fear gripped Lucy. For a few seconds she did not dare move. The thought of the bridge collapsing and dropping her into the drain with its writhing eels was bad enough. But the thought of the marsh itself opening a great crack, and herself and all the water and eels and reeds pouring into bottomless black, maybe right into the middle of the earth, was worse. She felt her toes curling like claws and the soles of her feet prickling with electricity.

Quickly then she began to walk – but it was like walking on a bouncy narrow plank between skyscrapers. She lifted each foot carefully and set it down firmly and yet gently. As fast as she dared, and yet quite slow. But soon – she couldn't help it – she started running. What if that earthquake shock had brought down the ceiling on her mother? Or even shaken the village flat, like dominoes? And what if some great towering piece of machinery, at the factory, had toppled on to her father?

And then, as she ran, it came again, pitching her off balance, so that her left foot hit her right calf and down she went. As she lay there, flat and winded, it came again. This time, the road seemed to hit her chest and stomach, a strong, hard thump. Then another. And each time, she saw the road gravel under her face jump slightly. And it was then, as she lay there, that she heard the wierdest sound. Nothing like any bird she had ever heard. It came out of the marsh behind her. It was a long wailing cry, like a fire-engine siren. She jumped up and began to run blindly.

Reading

1. Work with a partner. Read lines 1–24 again very carefully. Then answer the questions on **sheet 30**.

2. Work with a partner. Read the extract again very carefully. Then answer the questions on **sheet 31**.

Writing

PCM 33

1. Write part of a tense and scary story: **Meeting the Iron Woman**. Write in the first person.

2. Read your description to a partner. Which bits do you like best? Which bits could you improve?

Extended Writing

1. Revise your writing. Have you helped the reader to see what is happening, and to imagine how you are feeling? Add more detail where you need it.

2. Write another chapter of the story.

Don't forget!

- short sentences
- tension
- questions
- adjectives and adverbs
- precise detail
- see, hear, feel

13

EXPLANATION

How does it work?

Dudley showed me how a vacuum cleaner works

1 Vacuum cleaners are powered by a mini **motor** that runs on electricity. So, before switching it on, it needs to be plugged into a nearby socket.

2 WHIRRRR! Once the motor is running, it turns a fan round and round. As the fan spins, it pushes air out of the vacuum cleaner through a tube called a **duct**.

3 Because air is pushed out of the cleaner, air gets sucked in through the **head** to take its place, just like water being sucked up through a straw.

4 And as the air gets sucked up through the **hose**, so does the dirt and dust.

5 SSLLUUUUP! All this dust is then sucked up into a **bag**. But where does all the air go? It escapes through tiny holes in the walls of the bag. The dirt and dust are trapped inside – they're too big to get through the holes.

6 The bag fills up and after a while needs emptying or replacing. If you don't keep an eye on it, it becomes so full that it . . .

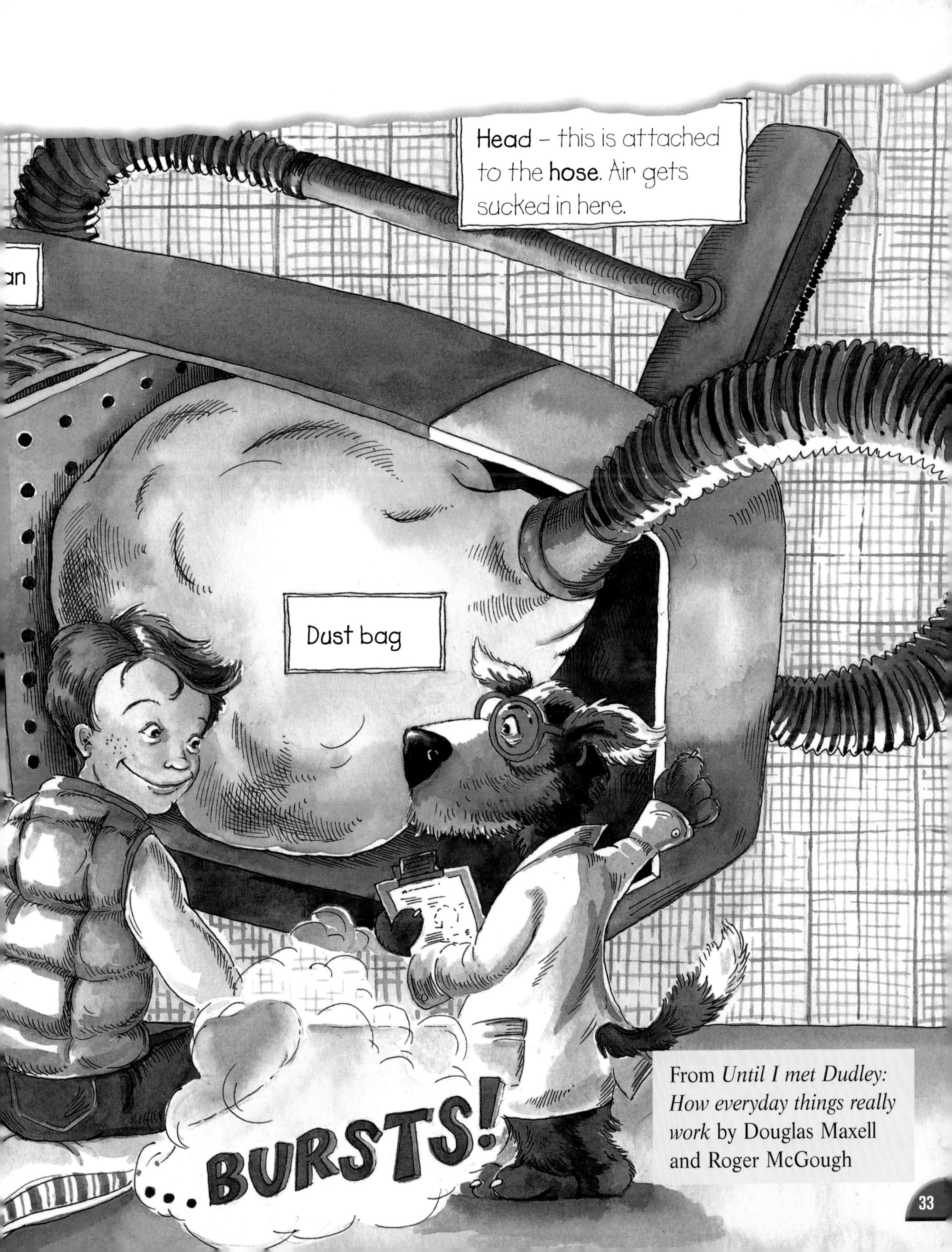

From *Until I met Dudley: How everyday things really work* by Douglas Maxell and Roger McGough

Reading

Work with a partner.

1. Draw and label your own diagram of a vacuum cleaner.

2. Using your own words, explain to a partner how a vacuum cleaner works. Point to the different parts of your diagram as you speak.

Writing

Work with a partner. Use **sheet 35**.

1. Finish the explanation from shared writing.

2. Use your homework drawing and notes to draft an explanation of how a simple machine works.

Extended Writing

1. Ask your partner to tell you how you can improve your explanation.

2. Write a final draft. Make sure your drawing/ diagram is clearly labelled.

EXPLANATIONS:

- numbered steps
- present tense
- connecting words
- labelled diagrams
- short paragraphs

14 SETTING

The Emerald City of Oz

When a cyclone hits her Kansas home, Dorothy is whirled away to the magic land of Oz. She follows the yellow brick road, and meets the Scarecrow, the Tin Woodman and the Cowardly Lion along the way. Finally she arrives at the wonderful Emerald City of Oz. The Guardian of the Gates gives them special spectacles so they won't be dazzled by the sight of the City . . .

Even with eyes protected by the green spectacles Dorothy and her friends were at first dazzled by the brilliancy of the wonderful City. The streets were lined with beautiful houses all built of green marble and studded everywhere with sparkling emeralds. They walked over a pavement of the same green marble, and where the blocks were joined together were rows of emeralds, set closely and glittering in the brightness of the sun. The window panes were of green glass; even the sky above the City had a green tint, and the rays of the sun were green.

There were many people – men, women, and children – walking about, and these were all dressed in green clothes and had greenish skins. . . . Many shops stood in the street, and Dorothy saw that everything in them was green. Green candy and green pop corn were offered for sale, as well as green shoes, green hats, and green clothes of all sorts. At one place a man was selling green lemonade, and when the children bought it Dorothy could see that they paid for it with green pennies.

Everyone seemed happy and contented and prosperous.

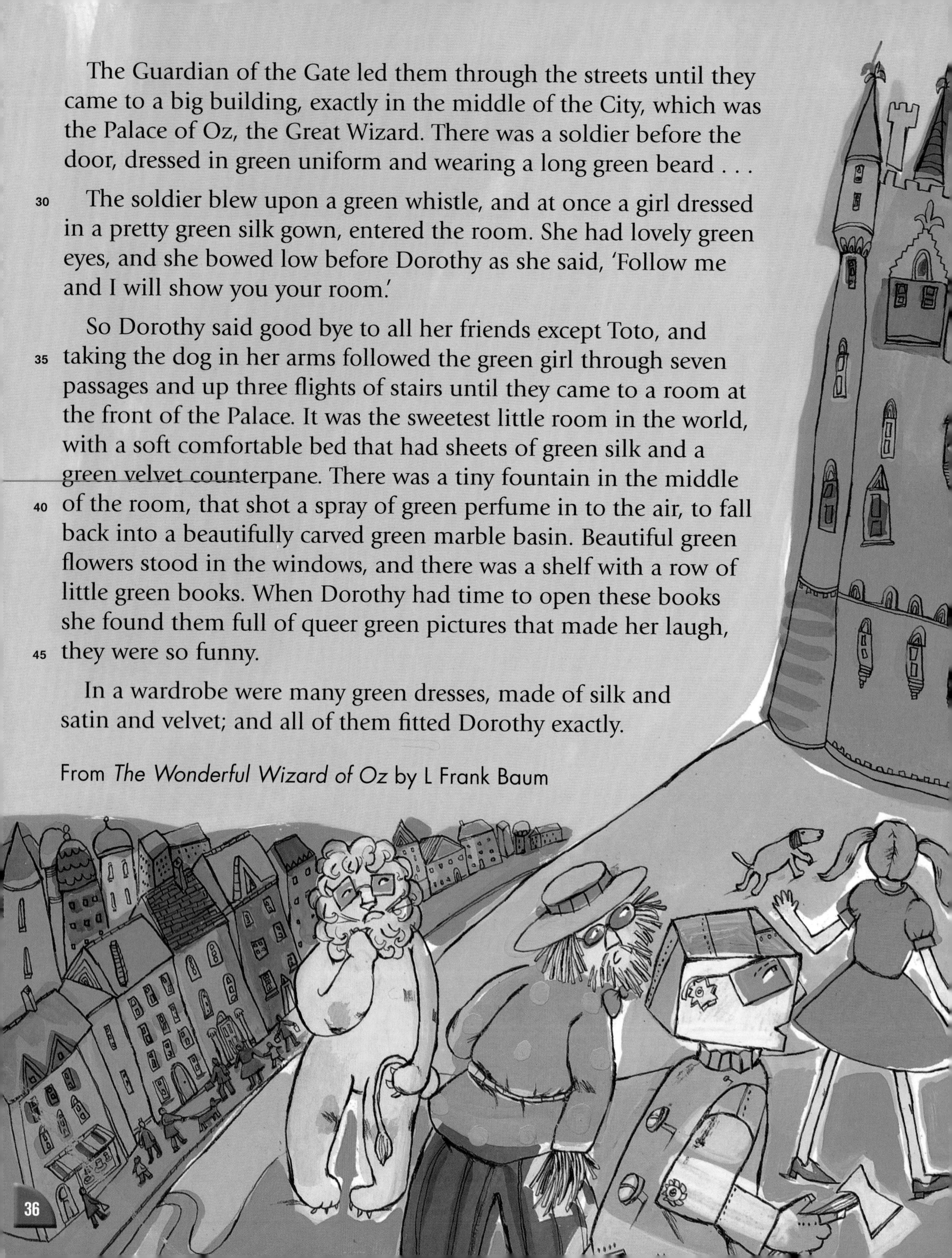

The Guardian of the Gate led them through the streets until they came to a big building, exactly in the middle of the City, which was the Palace of Oz, the Great Wizard. There was a soldier before the door, dressed in green uniform and wearing a long green beard . . .

30 The soldier blew upon a green whistle, and at once a girl dressed in a pretty green silk gown, entered the room. She had lovely green eyes, and she bowed low before Dorothy as she said, 'Follow me and I will show you your room.'

So Dorothy said good bye to all her friends except Toto, and
35 taking the dog in her arms followed the green girl through seven passages and up three flights of stairs until they came to a room at the front of the Palace. It was the sweetest little room in the world, with a soft comfortable bed that had sheets of green silk and a green velvet counterpane. There was a tiny fountain in the middle
40 of the room, that shot a spray of green perfume in to the air, to fall back into a beautifully carved green marble basin. Beautiful green flowers stood in the windows, and there was a shelf with a row of little green books. When Dorothy had time to open these books she found them full of queer green pictures that made her laugh,
45 they were so funny.

In a wardrobe were many green dresses, made of silk and satin and velvet; and all of them fitted Dorothy exactly.

From *The Wonderful Wizard of Oz* by L Frank Baum

Reading

Work with a partner.

1. What do you imagine Dorothy's room in the Palace of Oz is like? Make some notes, or draw and label a picture.

2. Re-read lines 1–29. Draw a map of the Emerald City, showing the gate, the streets and shops, and the Palace in the middle.

Writing

1. Imagine a magician's room. What is in it? What colours, sounds or smells are there? Make notes on **sheet 37**.

2. Draft a description of the room. Make it come alive.

3. Read it to a partner. Discuss how you could improve it.

Extended Writing

Draft a description of the magician. Plan and write a story about him.

Don't forget!

IMAGINARY SETTINGS:

- help the reader 'see' the setting
- use detailed description
- choose unusual words and phrases

RHYMING PATTERN

A Cautionary Tale

The Story of Augustus

WHO WOULD NOT HAVE ANY SOUP

Augustus was a chubby lad;
Fat, ruddy cheeks Augustus had;
And everybody saw with joy
The plump and hearty, healthy boy.
He ate and drank as he was told,
And never let his soup get cold.
But one day – one cold winter's day,
He screamed out – "Take the soup away!
Oh take the nasty soup away!
I *won't* have any soup to-day!"

repeated chorus

Next day begins his tale of woes;
Quite lank and lean Augustus grows.
Yet, though he feels so weak and ill,
The naughty fellow cries out still –
"Not any soup for me, I say:
Oh take the nasty soup away!
I *won't* have any soup to-day!"

The third day comes: Oh what a sin!
To make himself so pale and thin.
Yet, when the soup is put on table,
He screams, as loud as he is able,
"Not any soup for me, I say:
Oh take the nasty soup away!
I *won't* have any soup to-day!"

rhyming couplets

Look at him, now the fourth day's come!
He scarcely weighs a sugar-plum;
He's like a little bit of thread,
And on the fifth day, he was – dead!

tragic end

Heinrich Hoffmann

Reading

Work with a partner.

1. Read '**The Story of Augustus**' together. What does it have in common with '**Henry King**'? Make notes on **sheet 39**.
2. Practise performing '**The Story of Augustus**'. Divide the couplets between you.
3. Write down all the rhyming couplets used in '**The Story of Augustus**'.

Don't forget!
CAUTIONARY TALES:
give a warning
are humorous
use rhyming couplets
sometimes have a chorus
have a tragic end

Writing

PCM 40

Work with a partner.

1. Think of a wicked crime or habit.
2. Think of a name which rhymes with it.
3. Think of a horrible ending.
4. Start to draft your 'cautionary tale'. Clap out the rhythm as you work and revise it until it sounds right.

Extended Writing

1. Finish drafting your 'cautionary tale'. Read it aloud to your partner, and revise the rhythm and rhyme.
2. Make a final copy for a class display.

Robbers of the High Seas

Life on Board

The pirates' life was hard. They lived below deck in rat-infested quarters.

Many pirates died from horrible diseases such as yellow fever and scurvy.

They mostly ate hard-baked biscuits, fish and salted beef. When they ran out of fresh water, pirates drank beer, wine and rum.

Pirate Law

Although they broke the law of the land, pirates had their own strict code of behaviour.

THE PIRATES' ARTICLES

1 No pirate shall keep a secret, nor shall he run away.
Punishment: Marooning.

2 Pirates must keep weapons clean, ready for fighting.
Punishment: No share of treasure.

3 No pirate shall strike another.
Punishment: 39 lashes of the whip.

4 No pirate shall steal from a fellow pirate.
Punishment: Ears and nose to be slit and offender set ashore.

5 No pirate shall desert his ship in battle.
Punishment: Death.

6 No lit candles to be left unguarded.
Punishment: 39 lashes of the whip.

Don't forget!
NOTEMAKING:
jot down key words and phrases
make short notes
decide on headings

Reading

1 Complete the activities on **sheet 41**.

2 Scan the **'Pirates' Articles'**. Write brief notes about what pirates must and must not do.

3 Write down three questions that can be answered by reading **'Life on Board'**.

Writing

Think about your area of research.

1 What facts do you already know? Write them down.

2 What do you need to know? Write down some questions.

3 Scan the pages of your books to find answers. Jot down the key words only.

PCM 43

Extended Writing

Draft one or two paragraphs to go under your heading. You may want to use sub-headings.

STORIES FOR YOUNGER CHILDREN

Mr Creep the Crook

Allan Ahlberg

Mr Creep the crook was a bad man.
Mrs Creep the crook was a bad woman.
Miss Creep and Master Creep
were bad children,
and "Growler" Creep was a bad dog.

1

For some of the time Mr Creep
and his family lived in a secret den.
For the rest of the time
they lived in jail.

2

One day Mr Creep was sitting
in his little jail-house.
He was drinking a cup of jail-house tea
and eating a piece of jail-house cake
and planning how to get out.

3

Reading

1. Complete the activity on **sheet 44**.

2. What makes this story suitable for younger children? Write two sentences to explain your reasons.

Writing

Work with a partner.

1. Plan a simple story outline for your own 'Happy Families' story. You can continue the story from shared writing, or start a new one of your own.

2. Begin to draft your story together.

Extended Writing

1. Finish drafting your story.
2. Write it in a small book and illustrate it.
3. Design a cover and produce a final copy for a class collection.

Don't forget!

STORIES FOR YOUNGER CHILDREN:

- simple words and phrases
- short sentences
- repetition
- simple plot
- happy ending

18

NOTEMAKING

Talking to Rod Theodorou

Rod Theodorou has written several non-fiction books. In this interview he explains how he works.

Do you have to know a lot about a subject already before you begin to write a book?
I think it's much better if you do. It's very hard writing a book about something you don't know much about. If it's a subject you feel excited about then you will write in an exciting way. I've written four books about dinosaurs – that's my favourite subject!

How do you find out all the facts for your books?
In the past I always got lots of books out of the library to do my research. I still use libraries, but nowadays I also get a lot of information from the Internet. I read a lot and make notes. Then I work from my notes. I go back to the book or website if I need to check something.

How do you check your facts?
I check my facts by looking at lots of different sources. The publisher usually employs an expert to go through my manuscript as well.

Is writing non-fiction very different from writing fiction?
Yes. Writing fiction is like planting a garden – you don't know what bits will work and grow well, or exactly how it will look in the end. Writing non-fiction is more like building a house. You have to decide exactly what you want the book to look like beforehand.

Who do you write your books for?
I always write for primary aged children. For very young children you have to make sure each sentence is very clear. If there are difficult words these are usually included in the glossary.

Reading

Work with a partner.

1. Where could you find out facts for an information book on animals? Brainstorm all the places. Make notes.

2. Write down three key points about writing an information book.

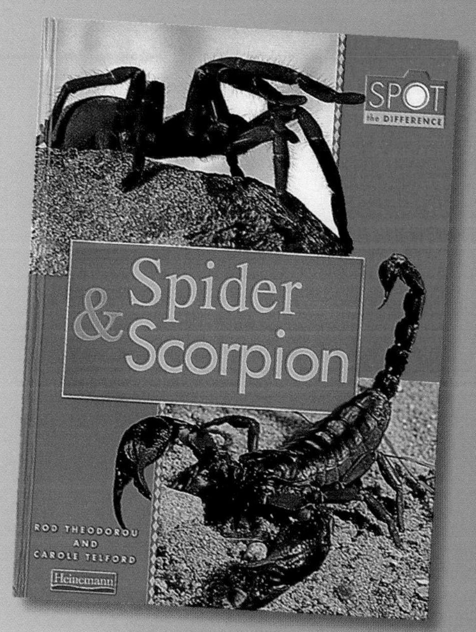

Writing

1. Work with a partner. Look through an information book together. Discuss 3 good things and 3 bad things about it. Make notes.

2. Look through an information book with a partner. Evaluate it using **sheet 46**.

3. Compare your book with another pair's book. Which is the best and why?

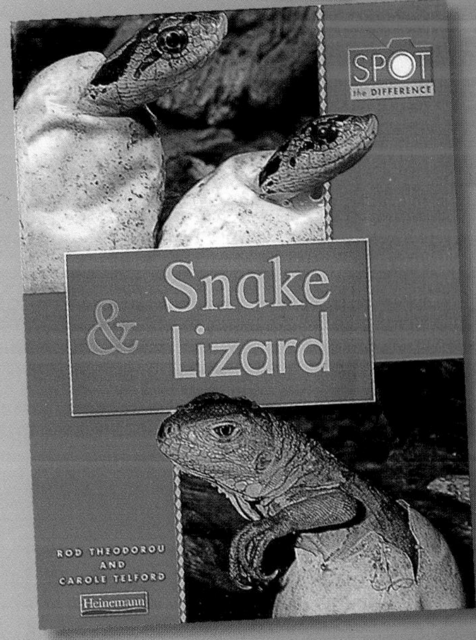

Extended Writing

Use your notes to write a review of your favourite information book.

NOTEMAKING:

- important facts
- key words
- abbreviations
- diagrams

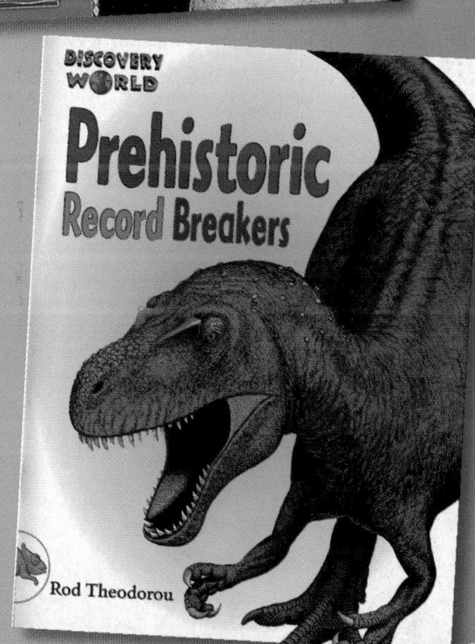

Snake and Lizard

Fact file

Lizard

Largest
The komodo dragon can grow up to 3 m long and weigh over 160 kg.

Smallest
The virgin gorda gecko is only 36 mm long.

Oldest known
One male slow worm (a sort of lizard) lived for 54 years.

This komodo dragon is eating a goat.

This reticulated py… is swallowing a dee…

Food
Most lizards eat insects. Big lizards eat meat. Komodo dragons eat animals as big as pigs and deer, and other dead animals. Some lizards just eat plants. The marine iguana eats seaweed.

Speed
The fastest lizard is the six-lined race-runner, which can run at 29 kph.

Snake

Longest
The reticulated python can reach between 6–10 m long!

Heaviest
The anaconda is almost twice as heavy as the reticulated python, weighing up to 227 kg.

Smallest
The thread snake measures only 108 mm long.

Oldest known
The longest lived snake was a common boa that lived for 40 years.

Food
Snakes eat meat – insects, frogs, lizards, fish and animals as big as a pig or a deer.

Speed
The fastest land snake is the black mamba. It can reach speeds of up to 19 kph.

23

Reading

Work with a partner.

1. Choose one animal each.
2. Brainstorm any facts you know already and write notes on **sheet 47**.
3. What else do you need to find out? Brainstorm and write questions on your planner.
4. Jot down any useful books. Write down any other places you could look.

Writing

Work with a partner.

1. Start to draft your fact file. Help each other to work out sub-headings. Use **sheet 48** if you want to.
2. Decide on your illustration and write a caption.
3. Start to design the lettering for headings.

Extended Writing

Finish your fact file. Think carefully about the layout and presentation.

- short sentences
- sub-headings
- facts
- captions

SIMILES

Red is like a trumpet sound

I asked the little boy who cannot see

I asked the little boy who cannot see,
'And what is colour like?'
'Why, green,' said he,
'Is like a rustle when the wind blows through
The forest; running water, that is blue;
And red is like a trumpet sound; and pink
Is like the smell of roses; and I think
That purple must be like a thunderstorm;
And yellow is like something soft and warm;
And white is a pleasant stillness when you lie
And dream.'

Anonymous

The writer of this poem

The writer of this poem
Is taller than a tree
As keen as the North wind
As handsome as can be

As bold as a boxing-glove
As sharp as a nib
As strong as scaffolding
As tricky as a fib

As smooth as a lolly-ice
As quick as a lick
As clean as a chemist-shop
As clever as a ✓

The writer of this poem
Never ceases to amaze
He's one in a million billion
(Or so the poem says!)

Roger McGough

Reading

Work with a partner.

1. Read the poem, '**I asked the little boy who cannot see**' aloud.
2. Complete the sentences on **sheet 49**.
3. Think of some similes to describe other colours – black, orange, brown.

Writing

1. Write your own similes poem. Use '**The writer of this poem**' as a model. Don't worry about making it rhyme.
2. Read it to your partner. Then revise it.

- 'see' the image in your head
- use descriptive adjectives
- compare things to other things

Extended Writing

1. Finish revising your poem. Does it sound right? Are the images clear?
2. Write out a final copy.

The Scrapyard of the Future

Did you know that old cars can be taken apart and recycled? Here's what happens:

STATION 1: the liquids

The oil and other liquids (petrol, water and brake fluid) are sucked out through a long tube.

They are stored in separate tanks.

STATION 2: the wheels

The wheels are screwed off.
The tyres and rims are separated.

Did you know?

Today's cars can be taken apart easily. The parts are numbered for quick sorting.

Did you know?

Lots of scrapyards are not fitted out for recycling, so lots of cars are just scrapped.

WHAT A WASTE!

STATION 3: the seats

The soft material and foam is cut off with a sharp knife.

SCIENCE GAME

How long does it take to take a car apart?

half an hour?

half a day?

a day?

STATION 6: the body

What's left of the car is smashed up by high-power hammers.

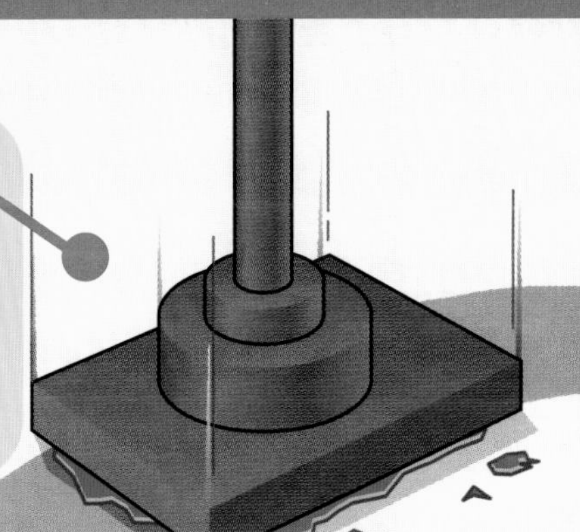

STATION 4: the windows

The glass windows (side and back) are cut out. The windscreen is a different kind of glass. It is taken out and stored separately.

STATION 5: the plastic parts

The bumpers and trims are taken off and sorted into different types of plastic.

WHAT CAN YOU DO WITH 1,000 KG OF CAR?

A car weighs about 1,000kg and almost all of it can be recycled.

PART	WEIGHT	HOW IT IS USED
Glass	35 kg	bottles, jars, glass-fibre
Plastic	85 kg	fuel for factory furnaces
Aluminium	54 kg	made into new car parts
Lead	5 kg	new car batteries
Steel	760 kg	melted down to make new car parts
Rubber	40 kg	road surfacing
Foam rubber	8 kg	carpet backing

Reading

1. Say what the extract is about in one or two sentences.
2. What two things happen to the **plastic** parts? Write down the key words only.
3. What is needed at Station 1 and Station 6? Use the pictures to help you.
4. Scan the chart. Which material is used to make new car batteries?

Writing

Working in a group, write a section for the class wall-chart.

1. Use books and other sources to find out information. Make notes of the key facts.
2. Select the information you need. Discuss how you are going to present it.
3. Draft your section of the chart.

Extended Writing

1. Finish drafting your section of the chart. Swap it with another group. Is it clear?
2. Revise it and present it neatly for the class wall-chart. Make careful drawings or diagrams if they will help.

- headings
- key words and facts
- suitable verbs
- drawings or diagrams
- captions

SOCIAL ISSUES

Jason and the School Bully 1

CHAPTER ONE

Jason's Last Defeat Ever happened one day when the school bully stopped him on the way home.

'Hello Craig,' Alistair said, trying not to give Craig an excuse to pick on him.

5 'What're you kicking?' Craig demanded.

clues about character

'Nothing,' Alistair said quickly.

'You must be stupid kicking nothing,' Craig laughed at him.

Alistair laughed too. Jason tried to look as though he was thinking of something else. If he copied Craig he'd be dragged
10 into his army of slaves.

Craig swung his bicycle in a circle in the empty road.

'Shut up!' Jason hissed at Alistair, when Craig had his back to them. He rode up beside them again.

'That's a great bike,' Alistair said, giggling nervously.

15 Jason thrust his hands into his pockets. He felt a pencil, string, shells from the beach, a penknife, last year s conkers.

'It's German,' Craig told them. 'Their bikes are better than the English ones.'

'How do you go so slowly?' Alistair asked.

20 'I've got a fixed wheel.'

'Can't you get it repaired?' Jason asked, to show he didn't think the bike was so wonderful.

'You're a cheeky little dwarf, Jason.' Craig looked down from his saddle. 'What are you?'

25 'Dwarf sounds like a sort of animal,' Alistair said giggling again.

'My dad says we all look like some animal.' Craig tossed his head to get his hair out of his eyes.

'What am I?' Alistair asked.

'Alistair the alligator,' Craig said, then added nastily, 'without any teeth.'

30 'What are you?' Jason asked before he could stop himself.

'My dad calls me tiger.'

'Sullivan the skunk,' Jason muttered.

Craig did not seem to hear. 'What about Jason, Alistair?' he asked. 'What about Jason the giraffe?'

35 Alistair laughed, hoping to please Craig.

'What's your other name, giraffe?'

'Smith,' Jason replied, feeling ashamed at saying his name.

'Smith's nothing. What's your middle name?'
40 Craig asked with a sneering smile.

'I've not got one.'

'It's Peter,' Alistair told him.

'Peter the puppy,' Craig said, trying it out. 'Still not small enough.'

45 'He's got a panda at home.' Alistair knew everything about Jason.

'You wait,' Jason promised, clenching his fists round conkers and shells.

50 'Peter the panda,' Craig cried in triumph.

Alistair gave a shrill laugh.

An extract from *Jason and the School Bully* by Eric Johns

Reading

1. Work with a partner. Do the activities on **sheet 52**.

2. Find three clues that tell you Alistair is scared of Craig.

3. Which of the three boys would you choose as a friend. Why?

Writing

What happens next? Plan and draft the rest of the story. Use **sheet 53** to help you.

Extended Writing

1. Finish the first draft of your story. Read it through with a partner. Is it convincing?

2. Make any changes then check each other's spellings and punctuation.

Don't forget!

- **How do the characters feel?**
- **What do they do?**
- **What do they say?**
- **What happens in the end?**

EXTENDED STORY

Jason and the School Bully 2

Alistair gave a shrill laugh.

'It's old,' Jason tried to explain, 'on top of a cupboard . . .'

'Do 'oo take your lovely pandy-wander to beddy-byes with 'oo?' Craig and Alistair slapped their sides, pretending to be helpless with laughter. 'Hey, Alistair, what do you think of this? Is it small enough? Peter the panda puppy! Panda puppy! Panda pup…'

Jason stretched out both hands and charged at the blurred shape on the bike. He could not stop the tears coming into his eyes and was furious at the thought that Craig might see them.

His charge took Craig by surprise, and he crashed down in the road.

'Now you've asked for it!' Craig yelled.

Jason saw the fuzzy shape of the bike on its side and, without thinking, jumped on the spokes.

'Stop him, Alistair, you stupid fool!' Craig screamed, stuck half under his bike.

Alistair caught hold of Jason's arm and tried to drag him away. Then his foot slipped off the kerb, and Jason swung him round and flung him on top of the bike.

He threw the conkers and shells at them and ran.

'Wait till I get you, Jason. I'll kill you for this. Wait till tomorrow!' Craig shrieked, choking back sobs.

CHAPTER TWO

The next morning Jason stayed in bed and pretended to be ill. He was too scared to go to school.

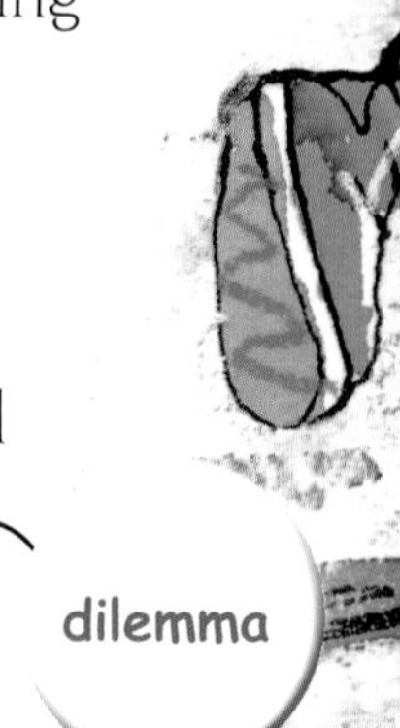

An extract from *Jason and the School Bully* by Eric Johns

Reading

Work with a partner. Look at the four pictures on **sheet 54**.

1. Fill in the chart to show what happened.
2. What could the character have done instead? Write this in the space provided.

Writing

1. Plan your own chapter story about a dilemma. Use **sheet 56**. Link each chapter to the one before.
2. Read your partner's plan. Is the dilemma clear? Does the story have a good ending?
3. Begin to write a first draft of your story.

Don't forget!
dialogue
action
motivation
difficult choices
resolution

Extended Writing

1. Continue writing the first draft of your story. Swap your work with a partner and make changes if needed.
2. Write out a final version of the story.

POINT OF VIEW

IT'S NOT FAIR!

Our class have been debating whether football should only be allowed to be played in the school playground on Mondays, Wednesdays and Fridays because our playground is quite small in the winter when we can't use the field.

show both sides

The people who don't like playing football say it is unfair that football takes up a lot of space in the playground. They say they cannot walk around because they get bumped into and hit with the ball. They also say it is scary for the little kids.

On the other hand, the footballers say that most people like playing so they should be allowed to. And if they cannot practise the school team will get worse and we won't win many games. Also they will not enjoy school if they cannot play with their friends.

summarise own point of view

I think football should be allowed every day because most people like it and it is good fun.

Paul, age 9

Reading

1. Read through the extract again. Do you agree or disagree with the writer's point of view? Make a list of the reasons why.

2. Write out a summary of your point of view.

   I think .... because ....

Writing

Work with a partner. Choose an issue together.

1. Make a list of the points for and against it using **sheet 57**.

2. Decide who you will present your argument to. Start to draft your argument.

PCM 58

Don't forget!

POINT OF VIEW:

- introduce the debate
- say what other people think and why
- say what you think and why
- summarise your point of view

Extended Writing

Revise and redraft your argument. Present it to a real audience if possible.

It wasn't a brick...

A young boy called Sausage has to face a dilemma at his swimming lesson in the local ponds. He has to dive down deep to the muddy bottom and pick up a brick. He's a good swimmer but he can't see without his glasses so he hates diving. All the other children watch as he goes in after the brick. He finds it, but he's scared, and desperate for air. When he finally reaches the surface and puts on his glasses he gets a surprise...

Because it wasn't a brick. It was just about the size and shape of one, but it was a tin – an old, old tin box with no paint left on it and all brown-black slime from the bottom of the Ponds. It was as heavy as a brick because it was full of mud. Don't get excited, as
5 we did: there was nothing there but mud. We strained all the mud through our fingers, but there wasn't anything else there – not even a bit of old sandwich or the remains of bait. I thought there might have been, because the tin could have belonged to one of those old chaps that have always fished at the other
10 end of the Ponds. They often bring their dinners with them in bags or tins, and they have tins for bait, too. It could have been dropped in to the water at their end of the Ponds and got moved to our end with the movement of the water. Otherwise I don't know how that tin box can
15 have got there. Anyway, it must have been there for years and years, by the look of it. When you think, it might have stayed there for years and years longer; perhaps stayed sunk under-water for ever.

I've cleaned the tin up and I keep it on the
20 mantelpiece at home with my coin collection in it. I had to duck-dive for another brick, and I got it all right, without being frightened at all; but it didn't seem to matter as much as coming up with the tin. I shall keep the tin as long as I live, and I might
25 easily live to be a hundred.

An extract from *Return to Air* by Philippa Pearce

Work with a partner.

Read the extract on **sheet 59** aloud. Then discuss the questions. Jot the answers down as notes.

Writing

Work with a partner. Use your homework notes to help you.

1. Decide what Sausage finds and how it got there. (paragraph 1)
2. What is he going to do with it? (paragraph 2)
3. Write a first draft of your alternative ending. Think of a good line to round off the story.
4. Read the draft through together. How can you improve it?

PCM 61

Extended Writing

Write a different beginning for the story – one which fits with your alternative ending.

- write two paragraphs only
- don't introduce a new plot line

ADVERTISEMENTS

SPECIAL OFFER!

FASCINATING FACTS ABOUT ALL YOUR FAVOURITE FOOTBALL STARS
There's now an easier way to collect your favourite players ...
Special offer!
Buy 2 packs get 1 free!
Offer ends 31 Dec
... just ask your newsagent.
Collectable football cards from HACKER

Reading

Work with a partner.

1. Look at the advertisements written by children on **sheet 62**. Which of the persuasive techniques are used? Fill in the chart.
2. Discuss how you could improve the adverts.

Writing

Work with a partner.

1. Discuss ideas, words and phrases for advertising yourself. Make notes.
2. Make a rough draft for your own advertisement. Use **sheet 63** if you want to.
3. Show it to your partner. Have you used all the key features? Is it persuasive?

Extended Writing

Continue to revise and polish your advert. Make a final neat copy. Think carefully about layout, lettering and colour.

Don't forget!
ADVERTS:
capital letters
catchy phrases
special offers
alliteration

SENSES POEM

Childhood Tracks

Eating crisp fried fish with plain bread.
Eating sheared ice made into 'snowball'
with syrup in a glass.
Eating young jelly-coconut, mixed
with village-made wet sugar.
Drinking cool water from a calabash gourd
on worked land in the hills.

Smelling a patch of fermenting pineapples
in stillness of hot sunlight.
Smelling mixed whiffs of fish, mango, coffee,
mint, hanging in a market.
Smelling sweaty padding lifted off a donkey's back.

Hearing a nightingale in song
in moonlight and sea-sound.
Hearing dawn-crowing of cocks, in answer
to others around the village.
Hearing a distant braying of a donkey
in a silent hot afternoon.
Hearing palmtrees' leaves rattle
on and on at Christmas time.

Seeing a woman walking in loose floral frock.
Seeing a village workman with bag and machete
under a tree, resting, sweat-washed.
Seeing a tangled land-piece of banana trees
with goats in shade cud-chewing.
Seeing a coil of plaited tobacco
like rope, sold, going in bits.
Seeing children playing in the schoolyard
between palm and almond trees.
Seeing children toy-making in a yard
while slants of evening's dusky hour lit up
by dotted lamplight.
Seeing fishing nets repaired between canoes.

James Berry

Reading

Work with a partner.

1. Using **sheet 64** make a sense web for the poem.
2. Add in some ideas for 'touching' on your sense web. Link them to other things mentioned in the poem.

Writing

Write your own senses poem called '**Home from School**'.

1. Talk about your ideas with your partner. Choose words that make the sights and sounds and smells and tastes seem real.
2. Start to draft your senses poem.

PCM 66

Extended Writing

1. Swap draft poems with a partner. As you read their poem concentrate on the images. Are they powerful? How could the poem be improved? Make one or two suggestions.
2. Produce a final, polished version of your poem for a class anthology.

Don't forget!
What can you:
hear?
see?
smell?
touch?
taste?

28 PERSUASIVE LETTERS

I'm writing to ask...

Dear Mum and Dad (the best parents in the whole wide world)

I really miss you. I'm not having a good time at Aunty Clare's at all and I can't get to sleep at night. She won't let me have the landing light on and my torch is no good because its battery has run out. Simon is horrible and teases me. He says I'm a wimp.

PLEASE PLEASE come and get me at the weekend.

Aunty Clare won't mind. I think she's fed up of having me here anyway because I don't like her cooking. Your cooking is just brill Mum and I wish I was there having tea with you right now.

Tons of love, please rescue me,

Anna

PS if you let me come home I'll make my bed every day AND DO THE WASHING UP!

make it sound a good idea for the reader too

Dear Mr Jenkins,

polite tone

I am writing to ask if I could possibly keep Mark off school next week because we have the chance to take a wonderful holiday in Spain.

I think it's very important to learn about the world by seeing it. I'll make Mark take some school work. I'm sure he'll benefit from all the new experiences.

I do hope you will agree to let him go. I know how important it is to attend school regularly but this is a chance in a lifetime.

Yours sincerely

Angela Lacey

Reading

PCM 67

1. Read through Mrs Lacey's letter.

   a Which is her most persuasive argument for keeping Mark off school? Why?

   b Which is her weakest argument? Why?

2. What other reasons could Mrs Lacey give to keep Mark off school? Choose one and write it out as a persuasive sentence.

Writing

PCM 68

Work with a partner. Write a persuasive letter.

1. Choose a subject that you feel strongly about.
2. Decide who you are going to write to.
3. Make notes for your argument.
4. Begin to draft your letter.

- polite tone
- clear arguments
- persuasive words and phrases
- connectives

Extended Writing

1. Finish drafting the letter. Swap it with another pair. How persuasive is it?
2. Revise and edit your letter, then write out a final version. Send your letter and see if it works!

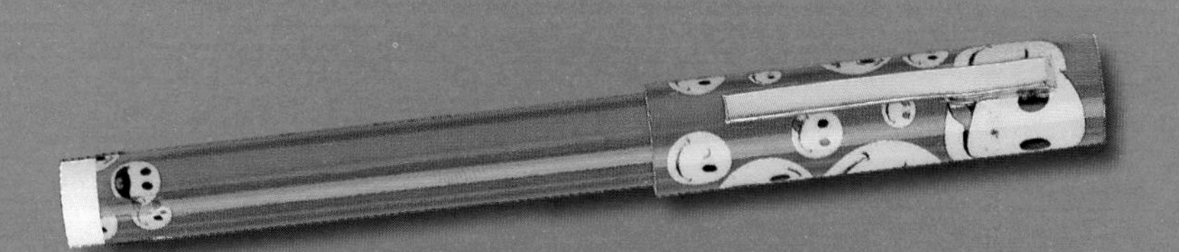

PLAYGROUND RHYMES

Skipping, Clapping and Counting

Skipping

Oliver-Oliver-Oliver twist
Bet you a penny you can’t do this:
Number one – touch your tongue
Number two – touch your shoe
Number three – touch your knee

Clapping

Have you ever ever ever in your long-legged life
Seen a long-legged sailor with a long-legged wife?
No I’ve never never never in my long-legged life
Seen a long-legged sailor with a long-legged wife!

Counting

Ibble obble
Biggle bobble
Ibble obble sprout
Wash the dirty dishcloth
Turn it inside out.
Ibble obble
Biggle bobble
Ibble obble OUT

Reading

Work with a partner. Use **sheet 69**.

Write the rest of the skipping rhyme. Think of words to rhyme with the other numbers.

Work out actions to go with it.

Writing

Work with a partner.

1. Make up a playground rhyme of your own.
2. Read your rhyme aloud to each other as you write. Will it be easy to remember?
3. Make up some actions to go with it.

Extended Writing

Continue to work on your rhyme. Revise and polish it until it's good enough for the class collection.

30

POINT OF VIEW

My Favourite Author

My favourite author is R.L. Stine. His Goosebumps books are spooky and mysterious. One good thing is when you get to the end of one book you know you can get another.

The one I like best is The Abominable Snowman. It says on the cover 'Reader Beware You're in for a scare'. And that's true. You really are. I think it is excellent using describing words which make you feel like you're actually in the story.

The setting is in Alaska. The characters are Jordan and Nicole. Their dad takes them for a holiday in the mountains where they find some ENORMOUS footprints. My best bit is where the dogs are really scared by something and their fur stands up on end and they howled and you know the monster must be coming . . . ARGHHH!

My favourite words are on page 73 – 'He loomed over us. He stood upright like a human, covered in brown fur.' And then there is more about the monster on page 75 – 'His lips were thick and white and set in a mean-looking grimace'.

Daniel, age 9

Reading

1. What are your reading habits? Finish the sentences on **sheet 70**.
2. Share your answers with a partner.
3. Make a list of books by your favourite authors. Check titles and publishers in the school or class library.

Writing

Plan a presentation about a favourite author. Work with a partner.

1. Choose an author you both like.
2. Start to plan your presentation. Make notes on **sheet 72**.
3. What props will you need (e.g. books, quotes, pictures)?
4. Decide who will say which part.

Extended Writing

Practise giving your presentation out loud. Revise your notes. Prepare your props.

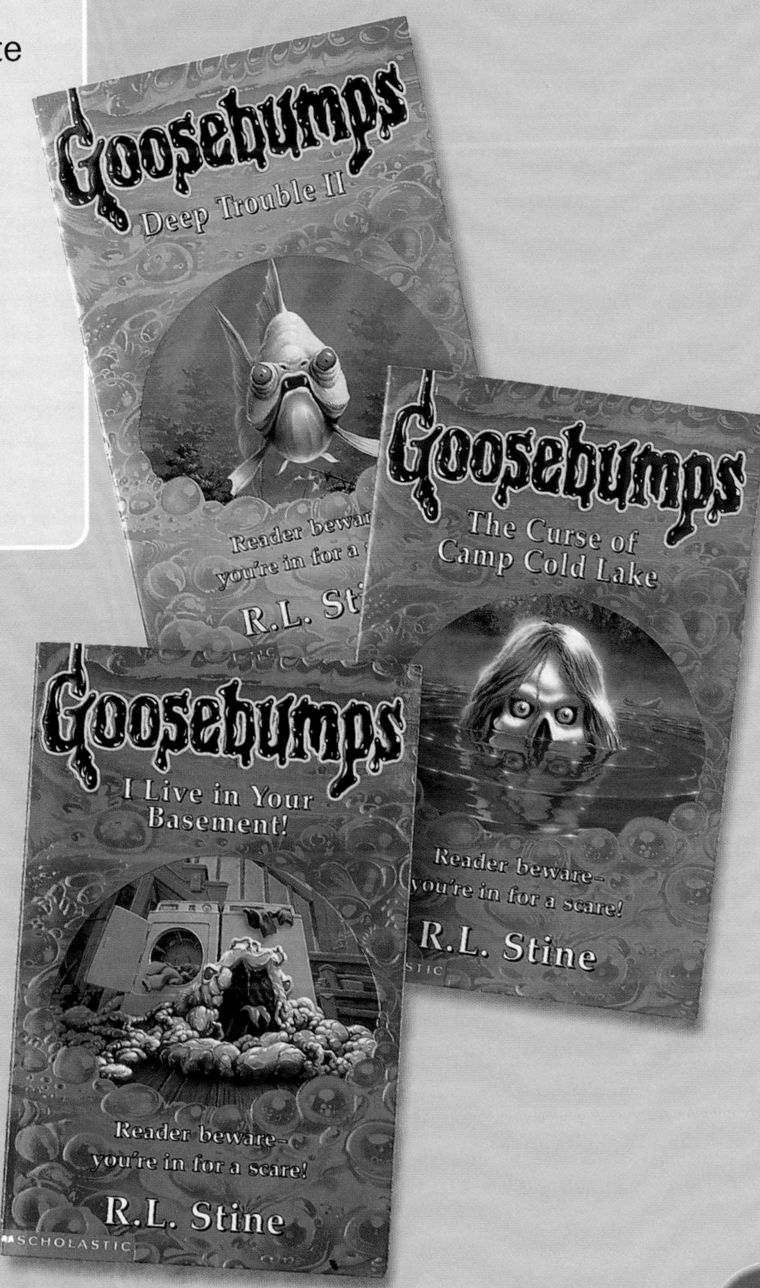

Acknowledgements

The publisher would like to thank the following for permission to use their copyright material.

TEXT
Unit 1: two extracts from *Boy* by Roald Dahl (Jonathan Cape & Penguin Books Ltd), reproduced by permission of David Higham Associates Ltd; two extracts from *Keeping Henry* by Nina Bawden (Puffin, 1989) © Nina Bawden, 1987, reproduced by permission of Penguin Books Ltd; **Unit 4**: from *Fantastic Mr Fox: A Play* by Roald Dahl and Sally Reid (Penguin Books Ltd), reproduced by permission of David Higham Associates Ltd; **Unit 5**: extract from *Ace Dragon Ltd* by Russell Hoban (Jonathan Cape, 1980) reproduced by permission of David Higham Associates; **Unit 6**: from *Tom's Private War* by Robert Leeson (Puffin, 1998) © Robert Leeson, 1998, reproduced by permission of Penguin Books Ltd; **Unit 7**: from *Beaver Towers* by Nigel Hinton (Puffin, 1995) © Nigel Hinton, 1980, reproduced by permission of Penguin Books Ltd; **Unit 9**: text reproduced by permission of *Young Archaeologist Magazine*; **Unit 12**: from *The Iron Woman* by Ted Hughes (Faber & Faber Ltd), reproduced by permission of Faber & Faber Ltd; **Unit 13**: from *Until I met Dudley: how everyday things really work* by Douglas Maxell and Roger McGough (Frances Lincoln Ltd) © Frances Lincoln Ltd, 1997 and reproduced by permission; **Unit 14**: from *The Wonderful Wizard of Oz* by L Frank Baum, first published 1900; **Unit 16**: from *Ships, Sailors and the Sea* (Usborne Publishing Ltd) © Usborned Publishing Ltd 1988, 1992 and reproduced by permission; **Unit 17**: from *Mr Creep the Crook* by Allan Ahlberg, illustrated by Andre Amstutz (Viking, 1998), text © Allan Ahlberg, 1998, illustrations © Andre Amstutz, 1998, reproduced by permission of Penguin Books Ltd; **Unit 20**: 'The Writer of this Poem' © Roger McGough, from *Poems for 9 Year Olds and Under* by Kit Wright, reproduced by Peters, Fraser and Dunlop Group Ltd on behalf of Roger McGough; **Units 22/23**: from *Jason and the School Bully* by Eric Johns (Corgi, a division of Transworld Publishers), © Eric Johns and reproduced with permission; **Unit 25**: from 'Return to Air' in *What the Neighbours Did and Other Stories* by Philippa Pearce (Puffin, 1995), © Philippa Pearce 1964, 1969, 1972, reproduced by permission of Penguin Books Ltd; **Unit 26**: 'The Dandy – Fun Gums Advert' from *The Dandy* © DC Thomson & Co Ltd and reproduced with permission; **Unit 27**: 'Childhood Tracks' from *Playing a Dazzler* by James Berry (Hamish Hamilton Ltd) © James Berry, 1996, reproduced by Peters, Fraser & Dunlop Group Ltd on behalf of James Berry.

ILLUSTRATIONS
Unit 1: artwork by Celia Witchard; **Unit 2**: photographs © Chris Honeywell; **Unit 3**: artwork by Lauren Foster; **Unit 4**: artwork by Clinton Banbury; **Unit 5**: artwork by Clinton Banbury; **Unit 6**: artwork by Shelagh McNicholas; **Unit 7**: artwork by Mary Claire-Smith; **Unit 8**: artwork by Beccy Blake; **Unit 9**: photo of girl © Keith Lillis, with thanks to the staff and pupils of Gallions School, London E6; photo of ruins © Tip/H Rogers; **Unit 10**: deer artwork by Alex Steel-Morgan; beetle artwork by Lizzy Finlay; **Unit 11**: map artwork by Andrew Warrington; photo © James Davis Travel Photography; **Unit 12**: artwork by Abigail Conway; **Unit 13**: artwork by Sarah Warburton; **Unit 14**: artwork by Joanne Davies; **Unit 15**: artwork by Lisa Williams; **Unit 16**: photo page 40 Mary Evans Picture Library and DTP artwork by James Sneddon; photo page 41 courtesy of the Ronald Grant Archive; **Unit 18**: photo courtesy of Rod Theodorou; **Unit 20**: page 48 artwork by Phylis Mahon; page 49 artwork by Melanie Mansfield; **Unit 21**: artwork pages 50-51 by James Sneddon; artwork page 52 by Clinton Banbury; **Units 22/23**: artwork by Lisa Smith; **Unit 24**; photo © Keith Lillis with thanks to the staff and pupils of Gallions School, London E6; **Unit 25**: artwork by Emma Chichester-Clark; **Unit 27**: artwork by Karin Littlewood; **Units 28/29**: photos © Keith Lillis with thanks to the staff and pupils of Gallions School, London E6; **Unit 30**: photo © Chris Honeywell.

Every effort has been made to trace all copyright holders. The publisher would be glad to hear from any unacknowledged sources at the first opportunity.